ENERGY FOR THE FUTURE AND GLOBAL WARMING

WATER POWER

By Andrew Solway

Consultant: Suzy Gazlay, M.A.,
science curriculum resource teacher

Gareth Stevens
Publishing

Please visit our web site at: www.garethstevens.com
For a free color catalog describing Gareth Stevens Publishing's
list of high-quality books, call 1-800-542-2595 (USA)
or 1-800-387-3178 (Canada).

Library of Congress Cataloging-in-Publication Data

Solway, Andrew.
    Water power / Andrew Solway.
        p. cm. — (Energy for the future and global warming)
    Includes index.
    ISBN: 978-0-8368-8404-3 (lib. bdg.)
    ISBN: 978-0-8368-8413-5 (softcover)
    1. Water power—Juvenile literature. I. Title.
    TC146.S65   2008
    621.31'2134—dc22   2007008754

This edition first published in 2008 by
Gareth Stevens Publishing
A Weekly Reader® Company
1 Reader's Digest Road
Pleasantville, NY 10570-7000 USA

Produced by Discovery Books
Editors: Geoff Barker and Sabrina Crewe
Designer: Keith Williams
Photo researcher: Rachel Tisdale
Illustrations: Stefan Chabluk

Gareth Stevens editor: Carol Ryback
Gareth Stevens art direction and design: Tammy West
Gareth Stevens production: Jessica Yanke

Photo credits: Bureau of Reclamation: cover, title page. CIV/DOD: / Gary Nichol 7.
istockphoto.com: / 10; / Geoff Kuchera 11; / Jack Morris 15; / Matej Michelizza 20;
/ Eric Foltz 29. U.S. Department of Agriculture: / 18. CORBIS: / Yann Arthus-Bertrand
24. Enwave Energy Corporation: / 26.

Printed in the United States of America

1 2 3 4 5 6 7 8 9 11 10 09 08 07

CONTENTS

Chapter 1:   Energy and Global Warming   4

Chapter 2:   An Ancient Source of Power   10

Chapter 3:   Hydroelectricity   14

Chapter 4:   Energy in the Ocean   22

Chapter 5:   Water Power for the Future   28

Glossary   30

Top Eight Energy Sources / Resources   31

Index   32

Cover image: Hoover Dam, on the Nevada-Arizona border,
was completed in 1936. The dam first produced electricity on October
26, 1936.

Words in **boldface** appear in the glossary or in the "Key Words"
boxes within the chapters.

CHAPTER ONE

ENERGY AND GLOBAL WARMING

Every day, the world needs more energy to keep things going. There are two main reasons for this increase in demand. First, there are more people in the world each day. Today, there are almost three times as many people as there were fifty years ago.

The second reason is that nations use more energy as they develop. The standard of living is changing in **developing nations**. People build more factories and buy more cars. They get heating for their homes. To power these things, people use more fuel and more electricity.

HOW ENERGY USE IS GROWING

People who live in countries in North America and Europe are rich compared to most of the rest of the world. They already use a lot of energy in their daily lives. Many countries on other continents are rapidly developing, however. Energy use in Asian countries — especially in China — is increasing by great amounts annually. Other countries in the Mideast, Africa, and South America will soon require their share of energy resources. By 2030, the world will need about twice as much fuel as in 2005.

Homes	22%	18%	Businesses
Vehicles	28%	32%	Power Plants

This chart shows energy use in the United States. It shows how much was used by homes, businesses, power plants, and vehicles.

Fossil fuels

Today, we get most of our energy by burning coal, oil, or natural gas. These fuels are known as **fossil fuels.** They formed from the remains of plants or animals that lived millions of years ago.

We use fossil fuels in several ways. Most **power plants** make electricity by burning fossil fuels. Cars, ships, and airplanes all run on gasoline, diesel, or other fuels made from oil.

In the past one hundred years, we have used up large amounts of the world's supply, or **reserves,** of fossil fuels. There are still huge reserves in the ground. But fossil fuels are not renewable. They cannot be replaced. Even energy experts do not know exactly how long fossil fuels will last. Coal, oil, and natural gas may run out at different times over the next three hundred years.

Pollution from fossil fuels

Scientists have shown that burning fossil fuels is polluting Earth. Pollution happens when harmful substances are put into the land, air, or water.

When fossil fuels burn, they produce **emissions** — waste gases that cause pollution. Coal is the fossil fuel that makes the most pollution. Oil, which we burn for heat and to run vehicles, also causes a lot of pollution. Pollution from fossil fuels can cause smog (a thick, dirty kind of fog). Fossil fuel emissions also cause acid rain, sleet, and snow. Scientists group all these under the term "acid rain." It can kill fish and damage trees and buildings.

Global warming

Burning fossil fuels also give off **greenhouse gases,** such as carbon dioxide and water vapor. Greenhouse gases trap heat in the atmosphere. They keep Earth warm enough for living things to exist. When too much heat is trapped, Earth gets warmer than usual.

The amounts of greenhouse gases in the air have increased in the last one hundred years. Scientists believe this increase is causing Earth to get warmer. This warming changes worldwide weather patterns, or the climate. This climate change is called **global warming.**

Renewable and clean

People are finding ways to reduce pollution and help slow global warming. If we use fewer fossil fuels, we will release less carbon dioxide

EFFECTS OF GLOBAL WARMING

Global warming is affecting the whole planet. At the North and South Poles, global warming is causing large ice sheets to melt. Water from the melted ice flows into the oceans and causes worldwide sea levels to rise. As ocean levels rise, coastal lands will flood. Global warming causes other changes as well. Some areas become too wet, while others becme too dry. As temperatures rise, certain regions may become deserts. Some regions now used for farming may become too hot and dry to grow crops.

In 2005, Hurricane Katrina flooded large portions of New Orleans, Louisiana. Scientists predict that extreme weather events, such as hurricanes, will become more common as global warming increases.

WATER POWER

GOOD THINGS	PROBLEMS
Cheap source of energy once system is built	Building **dams** and power plants costs a lot of money
Does not cause pollution or global warming	Not many places are suitable for large-scale dams
Works on a very large scale	People lose their homes when a reservoir is created; also causes massive habitat destruction
Energy can be stored	Fish and other water life can be harmed by dams
Supply can adapt quickly to demand	**Reservoirs** can fill with **silt** and become useless

into the air. This will slow down global warming. To reduce our use of fossil fuels, we must find other sources of energy. These sources need to be clean and renewable.

All around us, we have a source of clean, renewable energy — water. Water is already the leading renewable source of power. It does not produce greenhouse gases or cause global warming.

Wonderful water

The amount of water in the world is always the same. Some of it is in the air in the form of water vapor. About 2 percent is frozen solid in the form of ice. Most of Earth's water (97 percent) is in the oceans.

The force of moving water can be turned into mechanical energy — the energy to make things move.

THE WATER CYCLE

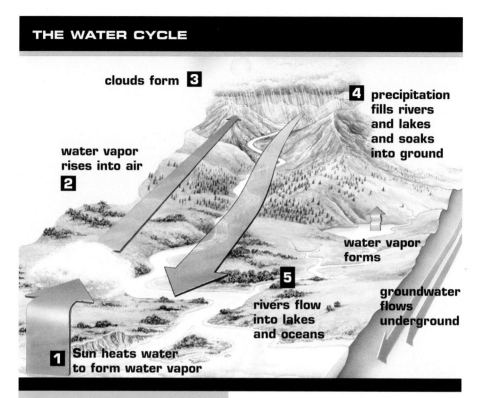

clouds form **3**

4 precipitation fills rivers and lakes and soaks into ground

water vapor rises into air **2**

water vapor forms

5

rivers flow into lakes and oceans

groundwater flows underground

1 Sun heats water to form water vapor

Water is recycled over and over again. (1) The Sun heats water to form water vapor. (2) This rises into the air. (3) Water vapor cools into droplets that form clouds. Clouds become too heavy to stay in the air. (4) Rain, sleet, or snow falls. (5) Water drains into rivers, which flow to lakes and oceans.

KEY WORDS

global warming: the gradual warming of Earth's climate
greenhouse gases: gases in the atmosphere that trap heat energy
reserves: fossil fuels that have not yet been taken out of the ground
silt: fine particles of soil that gradually settle on the bottom of a lake or river

For centuries, water has been used to power many things. Water will be an important source of energy for the future.

CHAPTER TWO

AN ANCIENT SOURCE OF POWER

Water power, or **hydropower**, has been around for a long time. More than two thousand years ago, people were using water to work machinery. They did this with **waterwheels** — wheels turned by the force of falling or running water. The first waterwheels may have been invented in the Middle East, India, or China. Many societies used them, including the ancient Greeks and Romans.

Types of waterwheel

Early waterwheels were set horizontally (flat) in the water. The current of the river or stream turned the wheel. It was connected to a large stone for grinding corn.

The force of falling water turns an overshot waterwheel and generates power. Water power is a free, renewable resource.

As a waterwheel turned, it turned the grindstone. By about 100 A.D., another kind of waterwheel was being used. This wheel was vertical (upright). Upright wheels produced more power.

Upright waterwheels can have either an overshot or an undershot style. Water falling from above turns an overshot wheel. This design is more **efficient** (produces more power) than an undershot wheel, which turns as flowing water pushes against the bottom of the wheel.

Using waterwheels

Throughout history, waterwheels have been used in many ways. The Chinese used them

CRAGSIDE HOUSE

In 1870, eleven years before the first power plant was built, Cragside House in Godalming, Britain, became the first building in the world to have electricity. The electricity was used to power arc lights (a kind of very bright electric light first made in the early 1800s). Cragside House used arc lights because the lightbulb had not yet been invented! Thomas Edison patented the lightbulb in 1879.

to power hammers hundreds of years ago. The hammers crushed rocks to make a powder used in porcelain. Arab peoples were skillful at harnessing hydropower. Waterwheels ground corn for flour, crushed sugar beets to make sugar, and pounded wood pulp to make paper. Europeans used waterwheels for those purposes — and to saw wood. Miners used waterwheels, too. They crushed rock to extract (remove) the metals.

From water mills to water turbines

The Industrial Revolution was the time when people first began using machines to make large amounts of goods. This period began in Britain in the 1700s. The Industrial Revolution spread from Britain to Europe and beyond. Hydropower was important in the early days of the Industrial Revolution. The first large factories were **water mills**. The water mills used hydropower to run the machines that made textiles (cloth).

Steam power soon replaced water mills in the Industrial Revolution. Hydropower did not disappear, however. During the 1800s, scientists developed new kinds of waterwheels, called water **turbines**. Waterwheels were large and turned slowly. Water turbines were smaller and turned at high speeds. Soon, water turbines were being used instead of waterwheels to power textile mills and sawmills.

Making electricity

In the late 1800s, people began using water turbines to produce electricity. Electricity made this way is called **hydroelectricity**.

The very first electric power plant was water-powered. It opened in Godalming, Britain, in 1881. A waterwheel in the river produced enough electricity for streetlights and lighting for a few buildings. The power plant soon closed because it was too expensive to run. Before long, many more powerful hydroelectric power plants appeared.

KEY WORDS

hydropower: power that comes from water's energy. (*Hydro* means "water.")
turbine: a type of engine powered by a flow of fluid. Turbines have large blades that spin, creating energy.
water mill: a mill (a factory with machines for processing materials) using machines that run on hydropower
waterwheel: a wheel turned by falling or running water

CHAPTER THREE

HYDROELECTRICITY

The use of hydroelectricity has grown fast since the 1800s. Today, hydroelectric power supplies about 20 percent of the world's electricity. In the United States, about 7 percent of the electricity comes from this source. Canada gets more than 70 percent of its electricity from hydroelectric power. Other countries get even more. Norway and Paraguay, for example, make nearly all their electricity from hydroelectric power.

How it works

Hydroelectric power plants need a source of flowing water. They are often built inside a **dam** that crosses a river. As the flow of river water backs up behind the dam, a **reservoir** forms. A reservoir is an artificial lake. People use reservoirs for recreational purposes, such as swimming, boating, and fishing. The reservoir may also provide water for farms, homes, and businesses. Reservoir water allows the hydroelectric plant to keep operating even if the flow of water in the river decreases.

Dams can be nearly any size. Those that contain power plants are usually massive structures, however. They must hold back millions of tons (tonnes) of water. Some are wide enough to allow a full-sized road to be built across the top.

HOOVER DAM

Dams are among the biggest structures built by humans. The Hoover Dam is on the Nevada-Arizona border near Las Vegas. It is 726 feet (221 meters) high. The dam was built across a deep canyon in the Colorado River between 1931 and 1936. The entire river was diverted through two huge tunnels while the dam was being built.

Hoover Dam — originally called the Boulder Canyon Dam — supplies power to roughly fourteen million people in the Southwest. A road runs across the top of the dam, which created Lake Mead.

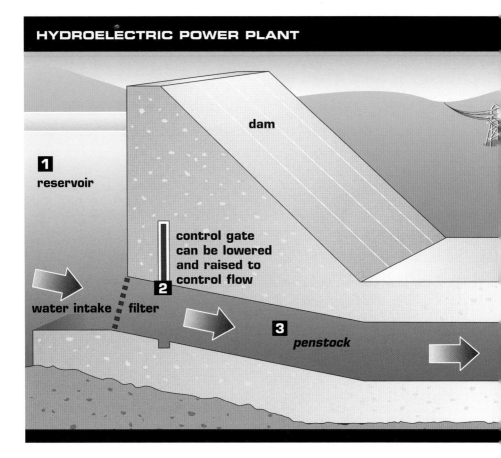

HYDROELECTRIC POWER PLANT

dam

1 reservoir

control gate can be lowered and raised to control flow

2

water intake · filter

3 *penstock*

Most dams are built across the narrowest part of a river. A dam's design depends on its location. Some dams rely on their great size to hold back the water and form a reservoir. Others use a curved shape to block water. The reservoir forms in what was the natural river valley.

A dam may also be a combination of designs. No matter the shape of the dam, however, any hydroelectric power plant within it works basically the same way. **Gravity** makes water flow downhill. The flowing water is used to produce electricity.

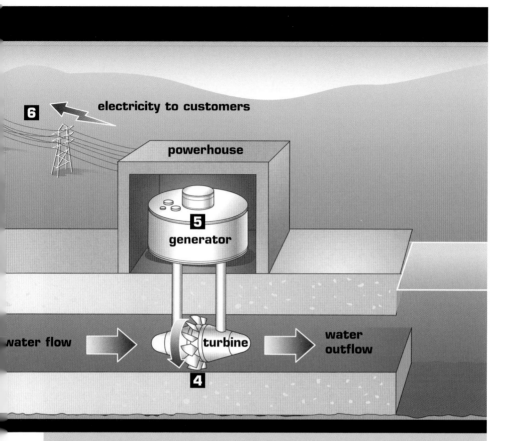

The dam for a hydroelectric power plant holds back water to create a reservoir (1). A control gate controls the flow of water. When the gate is open (2), water flows along the **penstock** (3). The force of the water spins the blades of the water turbine (4). The spinning turbine turns the **generator** (5). This produces electricity. Overhead electric power lines (6) carry electricity from the power plant to homes and industries.

Making hydroelectricity

Some kinds of hydroelectric power plants can be used to store energy as well as make it. This energy supply is known as pumped storage. The demand for electricity is always changing. It can be high at one time and low at another. When demand is

FISH FRIENDLY

Dams stop fish and other water animals from moving freely up and down a river. Turbines can kill fish. Scientists at the U.S. Department of Energy are working on the design of a new, "fish-friendly" turbine. Fish can swim right through this turbine and survive the trip. Many dams also have fish ladders for fish that need to swim upstream. A fish ladder looks like steps that run alongside a dam. Fish, such as salmon, can jump from one level to the next highest to move upriver.

Fish, such as salmon, can travel upstream around a dam by using a fish ladder. The fish keep jumping up or swimming from one step of the fish ladder to the next highest to reach the other side of the dam without injury.

low, power plants have extra electricity. This electricity can be used to pump water uphill into a second, higher reservoir. When the demand for electricity is high, the water in the higher reservoir is released. It rushes down through a turbine that makes electricity.

TOP DAMS

Most power:	China's Three Gorges Dam will produce 18,200 **megawatts** of electric power when finished in 2009.
Tallest:	Rogun Dam in Tajikistan is 1,099 feet (335 meters) tall.
Most material:	Syncrude Tailings Dam in Alberta, Canada, contains more than 700 million cubic yards (540 million cubic meters) of earth and rock.
Biggest reservoir:	Lake Volta in Ghana, Africa, covers an area of nearly 3,300 square miles (8,500 square kilometers).

Good and bad

Hydroelectric power seems like an ideal way to generate electricity. Water in rivers and lakes is constantly replenished by rainfall. Hydroelectric power is also free of pollution. Water turbines do not produce any polluting gases.

Large dams and hydroelectric power plants have some problems, however. Building a large dam is a huge task that takes many years. The costs are enormous. Once the dam is built, a large area of land is flooded to make the reservoir. People and wildlife have to move out of

The ancient temple of Ramses II, with its four enormous seated statues carved into rock, was originally built near Abu Simbel, Egypt. That area was flooded by the construction of the Aswan High Dam. Completed in 1970, the dam created a reservoir called Lake Nasser. In an enormous engineering feat, the temple was cut up and relocated to higher ground.

the area. More than one million people have lost their homes to make space for the Three Gorges Dam on the Yangtze River in China.

Dams also make the water flow more slowly. Silt and mud sinks to the riverbed. Silt can sometimes fill up a reservoir, making the power plant useless. The reduced flow can also affect water supplies for people downstream from the dam.

Low-head power

The **head** of a hydroelectric power plant is the distance the water drops as it flows through the plant. Power plants that produce a lot of electricity need a high head of water to work efficiently. Low-head power plants can still produce electricity, but not as much. They also do not need a large dam or reservoir to produce power.

Smaller power plants with low heads are built on smaller rivers. Such smaller hydropower plants do not cause a large reservoir to form. Instead, an underwater pipe upriver from the plant channels water into the turbine.

Most low-head power plants are considered micro (small) power plants. They produce only enough electricity to power a few homes. Micro-hydro systems can be built cheaply where other hydroelectric power may not work. Micro-hydropower is used in many countries. China, for example, has more than 85,000 micro-hydropower plants.

KEY WORDS

dam: a barrier to stop the flow of water

head: the distance water falls in a hydroelectric power plant

hydroelectricity: electricity made from water power

megawatt: a measurement of power produced. One megawatt is one million watts. A watt is the amount of electrical energy flowing in one second. Electrical energy is measured in units called joules. One watt is the same as one joule per second.

reservoir: a body of water that forms a lake behind a dam

CHAPTER FOUR

ENERGY IN THE OCEAN

Hydroelectric power is an important source of energy in many countries. There are other kinds of water power, however. These sources use the ocean's tides, waves, and stored energy. The energy in the ocean could supply power for the future.

Using the tides

Tides happen because of the regular rise and fall of sea levels. This change is caused mostly by the pull of the Moon's gravity acting on Earth. The Sun's gravity also pulls on the oceans somewhat.

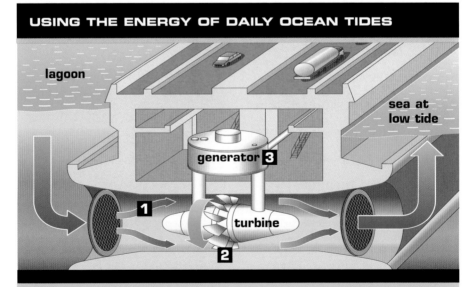

USING THE ENERGY OF DAILY OCEAN TIDES

At low tide, water in the **lagoon** is allowed to flow toward the sea through a turbine (1). As the water turns the turbine blades (2), the generator (3) makes electricity. At high tide, seawater flows back into the lagoon.

THE BIGGEST TIDES

The Bay of Fundy on the east coast of Canada has the world's largest tidal range. The water can rise and fall as much as 56 feet (17 meters). A location with such large tidal changes is a good place for a tidal power plant. A small tidal power plant has been built in the Bay of Fundy at Annapolis Royal. The location of that power plant has caused some erosion (wearing away) of the coast, however.

One way to use the power of the tides is to build a barrier across the mouth of a bay. The barrier has gates that open and close. It also contains turbines. As the tide comes in, ocean water flows into the bay through the turbines and generates electricity. The barrier's gates then close to keep the water inside the bay. When it is time for the tide to go out, the water flow reverses direction and pushes seaward against the barrier.

The gates then open, and water rushes out the opposite way, toward the sea. As water again flows through the turbines, more electricity is produced.

Certain areas on Earth have stronger tides than others. A tidal power plant needs a water level change of at least 16 feet (5 meters) between high and low tides. At present, there is only one large tidal power plant. It is at La Rance in France (*see page 24*). There are smaller plants in Canada, China, and Norway. New tidal power plants are being planned in many other countries, including Korea, Australia, Mexico, Russia, and the United States.

Tidal stream generators can also produce electricity from tidal flow. They use underwater propellers that get energy from the movement of water. Engineers must find ways to keep water plants and animals from being harmed by the propellers. Tidal stream generators are still very new, but they have great **potential**.

The La Rance River tidal power plant near Saint Malo, France, has been in operation for more than forty years. La Rance produces enough electricity to provide power to a large city.

Wave power

Another way to get energy from the ocean is to use the power of waves. Many people are experimenting with ways of using wave power. It is not as reliable as tidal power. So far, no major wave power plants have been built.

SALTER'S DUCK

In the 1970s, Professor Stephen Salter of Edinburgh University in Britain invented the "Salter's duck." Shaped like an aircraft wing, it made electricity from waves. The "duck" floated on the surface but was fastened to the seabed. It bobbed up and down on the waves. Its movements generated electricity.

Salter's design is still one of the most efficient wave-power devices ever invented. It can turn 90 percent of the energy of the waves into electricity. Salter's ducks are expensive to make, however. No power plant currently uses them.

Engineers have tried different ways of generating electricity from waves. One way uses a hollow, floating chamber that lets the waves flow in and out. When waves roll in, they push air up and out through an airshaft. The rushing air turns an air turbine (a kind of windmill). The turbine turns a generator that makes electricity. When the waves flow out of the chamber, air is drawn back through the turbine. This also produces electricity.

Other methods use devices that bob on the water's surface. They look like airplane wings, bobbing corks, or floating snakes. The "snakes" line up parallel with the waves and shoreline. The snakes are linked together by mooring lines that keep them straight. Snakes contain equipment that converts wave energy to electricity. The electricity travels to shore through cables.

Wave power plants must be located where there are large waves most of the time. They will need to operate in a wide range of weather conditions. Engineers hope to someday develop a good wave power system. Wave power plants could supply up to 5 percent of the world's energy. Like other kinds of hydropower, wave power is renewable and does not cause pollution.

Using ocean temperatures

The ocean collects huge amounts of energy each day.

Toronto, Canada, on Lake Ontario uses a system that cools office buildings near the waterfront. The system produces enough power to also cool nearly seven thousand homes in the surrounding area.

Even so, the Sun heats only the uppermost layer of the ocean. This means that the ocean is warm at the surface and cold deeper underwater. A process called **ocean thermal energy conversion** (OTEC) uses differences in water temperatures to create energy.

OTEC uses warm seawater from the surface and cold water from the ocean depths to power a turbine. The OTEC system uses several sets of pipes. One pipe contains the warm surface water. Another set holds liquid ammonia. **Heat exchangers** transfer the heat. Heat from the water pipes warms the pipes holding the ammonia. The liquid ammonia boils at a low temperature. It changes into a gas. The gas spins a turbine and generates electricity.

Next, another set of pipes comes into play. It holds cold water from the ocean depths. The cold water pipes cool down the pipes containing ammonia gas. The gas condenses into liquid ammonia, and the whole process starts over. OTEC is still an expensive way to produce electricity.

KEY WORDS

heat exhangers: a system consisting of sets of pipes that contain hot and cold liquids; the heat or cold transfers between the pipes to turn fluids to gases or gases to fluids

ocean thermal energy conversion: a process that uses the different levels of temperature in ocean water to make electricity

potential: future possibilities

tides: the regular rise and fall of ocean water levels that occurs twice daily

CHAPTER FIVE

WATER POWER FOR THE FUTURE

Today, water power is the most successful source of renewable energy. Making electricity from water is cheap and **efficient**. It also produces little pollution.

Small power plants and ocean energy

In the future, using more hydroelectric power will help reduce pollution and slow down global warming. There are limits to how many large hydroelectric plants we can build. But there are many places where micro-hydro systems can be used. They could supply a small area or even just one house. Micro-hydropower could greatly increase the amount of electricity we get from water.

People may someday get large amounts of energy from the oceans. Tidal stream generators and wave power could make large amounts of electricity. Floating OTEC power plants could produce a lot of energy, too.

There are still challenges facing the use of ocean energy. One of them is that saltwater causes **corrosion**. The salt slowly eats away at metal parts used in power plants. Scientists are constantly working on ways to solve these kinds of problems.

The energy problem

In the future, we will use several different forms of energy. Wind power and

Grand Coulee Dam, on the Columbia River, in Washington state is the largest concrete structure in the United States. The power plant has four powerhouses that produce up to 6,500 megawatts of electricity. It is the largest producer of hydroelectric power in the United States.

solar energy (energy from sunlight) will be important. **Biofuels** — fuels made from plant and animal matter — will also be part of the mix. So will hydrogen gas. By itself, hydropower could never completely replace fossil fuels. But it will play an important part in supplying our future energy needs.

KEY WORDS

biofuels: fuels made from biomass (material from plants or animals). Wood is a biofuel. Corn oil, restaurant waste, or other natural plant products can be used as biofuel.
corrosion: act of eating away at something
efficient: working well and without much waste

GLOSSARY

dam: a barrier to stop the flow of water

developing nation: a country that is starting to build industries, or industrialize. These countries usually have fast-growing populations. Many developing nations stayed poor while other nations in North America and Western Europe grew rich.

efficient: working well and without much waste

emissions: substances let out into the air, such as carbon dioxide given off by burning coal or oil

fossil fuels: fuels formed in the ground over millions of years, including coal, oil, and natural gas

generator: a machine that uses fuel to make electrical energy

gravity: an attractive force that pulls objects together. Earth, the Moon, and the Sun all pull objects toward themselves because of the force of gravity.

hydroelectricity: electricity made from hydropower (water power). It is also called hydroelectric power.

hydropower: power that comes from water's energy. (Hydro means water.)

lagoon: an area of water separated from the sea by a barrier

penstock: channel or pipe along which water flows to a turbine

potential: future possibilities

power plant: a factory that produces electricity

reservoir: a lake that forms behind a dam

TOP EIGHT ENERGY SOURCES

in alphabetical order

The following list highlights the major fuel sources of the twenty-first century. It also lists some advantages and disadvantages of each:

	Advantages	Disadvantages
Biofuels	renewable energy source; widely available from a number of sources, including farms, restaurants, and everday garbage	fossil fuels often used to grow farm crops; requires special processing facilities that run on fossil fuels in order to produce usable biofuel
Fossil fuels: coal, oil, petroleum	used by functioning power plants worldwide; supports economies	limited supplies; emit greenhouse gases; produce toxic wastes; must often be transported long distances
Geothermal energy	nonpolluting; renewable; free source	available in localized areas; would require redesign of heating systems
Hydrogen (fuel cells)	most abundant element in the universe; nonpolluting	production uses up fossil fuels; storage presents safety issues
Nuclear energy	produces no greenhouse gases; produces a lot of energy from small amounts of fuel	solid wastes remain dangerous for centuries; limited life span of power plants
Solar power	renewable; produces no pollutants; free source	weather and climate dependent; solar cells expensive to manufacture
Water power	renewable resource; generally requires no additional fuel	requires flowing water, waves, or tides; can interfere with view; dams may destroy large natural areas and disrupt human settlements
Wind power	renewable; nonpolluting; free source	depends on weather patterns; depends on location; endangers bird populations

RESOURCES

Books

Parker, Steve. *Water Power.*
Science Files: Energy (series).
Gareth Stevens (2004)

Petersen, Christine.
Alternative Energy.
True Books (series).
Children's Press (2004)

Web Sites

www.pbs.org/tesla/ins/niagara.html
View an animated diagram that shows how the Niagara River is used to make electricity.

www.eia.doe.gov/kids/energyfacts/ sources/renewable/ocean.html
Learn more about water power from the U.S. Department of Energy Web site that explores ocean energy.

Publisher's note to educators and parents: Our editors have carefully reviewed these Web sites to ensure that they are suitable for children. Many Web sites change frequently, however, and we cannot guarantee that a site's future contents will continue to meet our high standards of quality and educational value. Be advised that children should be closely supervised whenever they access the Internet.

Abu Simbel, Egypt 20
acid rain 6
Aswan High Dam, Egypt 20

Bay of Fundy, Canada 23

Canada 14, 19, 23, 24, 26
carbon dioxide 6
China 10, 11, 19, 20, 21, 24
corrosion 28
costs 8, 13, 19, 21, 25, 27, 28
Cragside House, Britain 12

dams 8, 14, 15, 16, 17, 18, 19–20, 21, 29
developing nations 4

Edison, Thomas 12
emissions 6
energy demands 4, 8, 17–18
energy use chart 5

fish ladders 19
fossil fuels 5–6, 8, 9, 29

generators 17, 22, 24, 25, 28
global warming 6, 7, 8, 9, 28
Godalming, Britain 12, 13
Grand Coulee Dam, Washington 29
gravity 16, 22
greenhouse gases 6, 8, 9

Hoover Dam 3, 15
Hurricane Katrina 7

ice 7, 8
impact on wildlife 8, 18, 19, 24
Industrial Revolution 12–13

La Rance tidal power plant, France 23, 24
lagoons 22

Lake Volta, Ghana 19
liquid ammonia 27
low-head power 21

mechanical energy 8
megawatts 19, 21, 29

ocean temperatures 26–27, 28
oceans 7, 8, 9, 22–23, 24, 26–27, 28

penstocks 16, 17
pollution 6, 8, 19, 26, 28
power plants 5, 8, 12, 13, 14, 16–17, 19, 20, 21, 23–24, 25, 26, 28, 29

renewable energy 5–6, 8, 19, 26, 28
reservoirs 8, 14, 16–17, 18, 19, 20, 21
Rogun Dam, Tajikistan 19

Salter's ducks 25
silt 8, 9, 20
storing energy 8, 17–18, 22
Syncrude Tailings Dam, Alberta, Canada 19

Three Gorges Dam, China 19, 20
tidal stream generators 24, 28
tides 22–24, 27, 28
Toronto, Canada 26
turbines 13, 17, 18, 19, 21, 22, 23, 25, 27

United States 5, 14, 18, 24, 29

water cycles 9
water mills 12–13
water vapor 6, 8, 9
waterwheels 10–12, 13
waves 22, 24–26, 28

Yangtze River, China 20